ONCE UPON A TIME IN CHINA

THE DREAMER OF STARS

JILLIAN LIN
Illustrations by SHI MENG

Zhang Heng (78–139), scientist, inventor, poet, and painter, Eastern Han Dynasty

Once upon a time in China...

... lived a boy called Zhang (*Jahng*), who loved gazing at the night sky. Every night, when it was completely dark, he went outside. He found a place to lay on his back. For hours and hours, he stared up at the bright moon and the twinkling stars. While admiring the night lights, Zhang asked himself many questions.

How many stars are in the sky? Why is the moon so bright? How did the sky and earth come about?

At the time, people in China thought the sky was round and the earth was square, with the sky moving around the earth. Zhang wasn't sure if that was true. He wanted to find proof so he said to himself, 'One day, I am going to find the answers to all my questions.'

Zhang was a clever boy. He was brilliant in mathematics and science, but he also loved writing stories and poems.

When he was sixteen, his mother sent him away to attend a famous school far from home. She wanted him to become a writer.

Zhang was sad to leave his family behind, but he soon made friends and enjoyed learning new things.

After he finished school, Zhang found a good job as a writer for the government. He worked very hard and became well known for his excellent reports. Soon, even the emperor of China heard about him. Zhang was offered a job at the palace as the emperor's Grand Astrologer.

Zhang was overjoyed. In his new job, he had to study the weather, the calendar, and natural events like

earthquakes and floods. What he liked most about the
work was that he also had to study the position and
movement of the stars.

Zhang got to work in the Royal Observatory, a special place dedicated to the study of the stars, moon, and sky. His work was top secret. It was so secret that if people talked about what was going on inside, their lives would be taken.

Zhang worked day and night counting the stars and studying how they moved. This went on for years and years. During this time, he counted close to 3,000 stars and gave names to the 300 brightest stars. He found out that the moon did not have light on its own, but that it reflected the light from the sun. From his findings, he drew a detailed map of the sky.

One night, Zhang was gazing up at the stars again when he started to mumble, 'The sky is moving around the earth, so the sky is like a ball with the earth in its center...'

He started scratching his head and suddenly he shouted, 'I've got it! The sky is not round, and the earth is not square, like people say. The sky is like a chicken's egg. Inside, in its centre, lies a round ball, just like the yolk of an egg.' He jumped up in joy.

'The earth is that ball. It is round!'

Zhang was very excited about his new discovery, but he was not happy with the paper maps he had drawn. That is why he invented a special machine that he used as a model of the sky. It was huge – more than 16 feet (five meters) from one side to the other.

The model had the earth at its center with the sun, moon, and stars moving around it. Zhang used this machine to study the universe and make new discoveries. Finally he was able to find answers to many of the questions he had had as a little boy.

The model of the universe was only one of Zhang's inventions. He also built a vehicle carrying a wooden figure that would always point to the south, whichever way it turned. It worked like a compass.

Another invention was a cart carrying a figure that would beat a drum every 0.3 miles (500 meters) it traveled. These two inventions were especially useful for soldiers in the army when they marched long distances across the country.

Zhang became especially famous for one invention. Throughout its history, China has suffered from earthquakes. Zhang was the first person in the world to invent a machine that could predict them.

The machine was in the shape of an egg with eight dragon heads around the top, each with a copper ball in its mouth.

Around the bottom, directly under the

dragon heads, were eight frogs.

When an earthquake occurred, a ball fell out of a dragon's mouth into the frog's mouth that was facing the direction of the quake.

One day, Zhang noticed that a copper ball had dropped in his machine. He immediately went to see the emperor and told him, 'Your Majesty, there has been a serious earthquake to the west of the city.'

The emperor did not believe him as he had not received any reports of earthquakes.

However, a few days later, a messenger came running into the palace, saying, 'Your Highness, there has been a big earthquake!' It had taken place more than 310 miles (500 kilometers) west from the palace.

Only then did the emperor believe in Zhang's clever invention.

Some people say that Zhang was the cleverest man in the whole history of China. He was not just a brilliant inventor, but he was also a master painter, a gifted poet, and a whiz in mathematics.

Surprisingly, he wasn't famous in his lifetime. Fame was not important to him. He was more interested in finding answers to his questions.

Even so, Zhang would have been proud to know that his name lives on in outer space: the Zhang Heng Asteroid number 1802.

The End

1 ~ Zhang was one of the first to come up with the idea of drawing gridlines (horizontal and vertical lines on maps) so it was easier to calculate where certain places were. This also helped to find out how far one  place was from another. The Chinese called it 'throwing a net over the earth'.

2 ~ After years of counting, Zhang found not only the bigger stars but he also added 11,520 small stars that Chinese sailors had spotted in the sky.

Zhang Heng's armillary sphere was used as a model of objects in the sky.

3 ~ Zhang used the power of water to make the earth in his machine of the universe spin around. It completed one turn every year, just like the real globe does. That was how he showed how the positions of the stars changed from one year to the next. It also showed how the moon grows from a curved shape to a round, full moon.

4 ~ Zhang was an expert in mathematics. He made calculations for an important mathematical number called 'pi' (π). Although his calculation was a little bit different from the pi we use today, it was very close. It was also 1,600 years before pi was officially invented.

5 ~ In Zhang's time, people thought that natural disasters such as floods and earthquakes were signs from above. They believed that the gods were unhappy with the emperor and the things he had done. That is why Zhang had to study the weather and the calendar – to tell the emperor if the gods were happy with him.

6 ~ Part of the earthquake machine Zhang invented were eight dragons hanging upside down. The heads of the dragons pointed to the directions of east, west, north, south, northeast, northwest, southeast, and southwest. When an earthquake happened, the shaking of the earth made a weight inside the machine swing toward the direction of the quake. A lever connected to the dragon of that direction caused its mouth to open. Out of the dragon's mouth dropped a bronze ball that fell into the frog's mouth, making a noise.

Model of Zhang Heng's seismometer to predict earthquakes.

7 ~ Zhang could have been a lot more successful. He turned down important jobs, even though he could have earned more money and become famous. Instead, he preferred to spend time away from the city to think about how the universe works.

8 ~ Zhang wrote poems about a lot of different topics, including history and the government, but also about love and beautiful places in China. This is how his famous poem *Four Sorrows* starts:

In Taishan stays my dear sweetheart
But the Liangfu mountain keeps us apart
Looking east, I find tears start
She gave a sword for me to call my own
In return I gave her a special jade stone
I'm so sad as she is out of sight
Why should I trouble myself all night?

Some people believe Zhang did not write this as a love poem. They think the poem was really about him and the emperor – Zhang could have been angry that jealous people blocked him from talking to the emperor.

*Chinese stamp of
Zhang Heng
(1955).*

9 ~ In another of his famous poems, Zhang wrote
about how his mind left his body, just like in a
dream. It traveled through space and looked at the
Earth as a round ball below.

10 ~ Apart from the asteroid, other things were named
after Zhang. They include the
Chang Heng lunar crater (a
bowl-shaped hole on the far side
of the moon) and the golden-
yellow mineral Zhanghenite.

TEST YOUR KNOWLEDGE!

1   When Zhang was a little boy, why did he like looking up at the sky at night?

a)   He thought the stars were going to crash into the earth.

b)   He wondered how many stars were in the sky, why the moon was so bright, and how the sky and earth had come about.

c)   He dreamed about flying to the moon.

2   What did Zhang have to do in his job as Grand Astrologer for the emperor?

a)   He had to write books for schools.

b)   He had to write long reports about the history of China.

c)   He had to study the calendar, natural events like earthquakes and floods, and the stars.

Answers to the Quiz: 1. b / 2. c / 3. a / 4. a / 5. c

3   What did Zhang use the model of the sky for, which he had invented?

a)   To study the universe and make new discoveries.

b)   To show people the earth was square.

c)   To put up as a decoration in his office.

4   Why didn't the emperor believe Zhang when he told him there had been an earthquake?

a)   Because he had not received any reports of any earthquakes.

b)   Because there were no earthquakes in China.

c)   Because Zhang could not explain to him what an earthquake was.

5   How can people remember Zhang today?

a)   A lunar crater is named after him.

b)   An asteroid is named after him.

c)   All of the above.

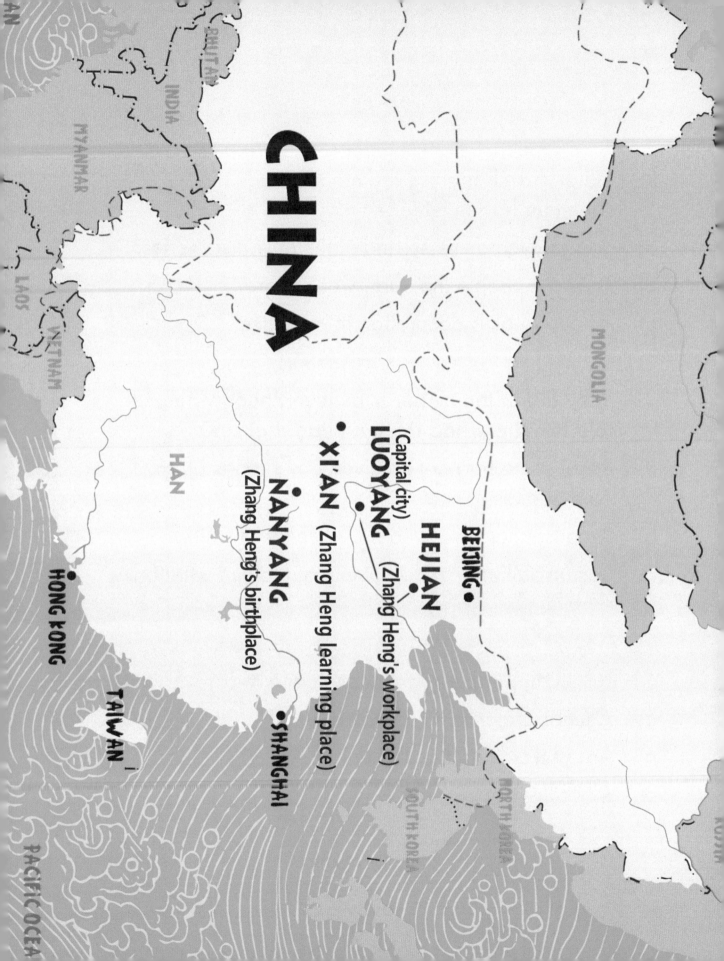

The *Once Upon A Time In China...* Series

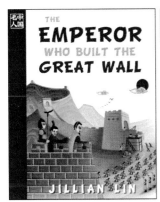

Qin Shihuang

Confucius

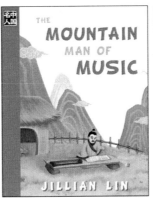

Zhu Zaiyu

Hua Tuo

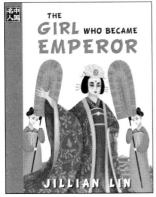

Wu Zetian

Zhang Heng

Zheng He

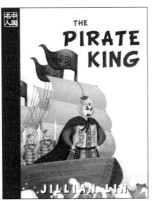

Koxinga

Also available as e-books. For more information, visit

www.jillianlin.com

The Dreamer Of Stars

Copyright © Jillian Lin 2016
Illustrations © Shi Meng 2016

Photo of seismograph: © Deror avi
Photo of armillary sphere: © Hans A Rosbach
Photo of stamp: © State Post Bureau of China
Photo of crater: © Arizona State University

Made in the USA
Columbia, SC
24 January 2022

54751639R00020